Thomas Edison

The Man Behind the Light Bulb

by Lucia Raatma

PEBBLE

a capstone imprint

Little Explorer is published by Pebble,
1710 Roe Crest Drive, North Mankato, Minnesota 56003
www.capstonepub.com

Library of Congress Cataloging-in-Publication Data
Names: Raatma, Lucia, author.
Title: Thomas Edison : the man behind the light bulb / by Lucia Raatma.
Description: North Mankato, Minnesota : Pebble, [2020] | Audience: Ages: 6–8.
 | Audience: Grades: K–3. | Includes bibliographical references and index. Identifiers:
LCCN 2018061610| ISBN 9781977109743 (hardcover) | ISBN 9781977110626 (pbk.) |
ISBN 9781977109842 (ebook pdf) Subjects: LCSH: Edison, Thomas A. (Thomas Alva),
1847–1931—Juvenile literature. | Inventors—United States—Biography—Juvenile literature. |
Light bulbs—Juvenile literature. | Electric lighting—Juvenile literature. | Electric lighting. sears
Classification: LCC TK140.E3 R34 2020 | DDC 621.3092 [B]—dc23
LC record available at https://lccn.loc.gov/2018061610

Editorial Credits
Erika L. Shores, editor; Kayla Rossow, designer; Svetlana Zhurkin, media researcher;
Tori Abraham, production specialist

Our very special thanks to Emma Grahn, Spark!Lab Manager, Lemelson Center for the Study of Invention
and Innovation, National Museum of American History. Capstone would also like to thank Kealy Gordon,
Product Development Manager, and the following at Smithsonian Enterprises: Ellen Nanney, Licensing
Manager; Brigid Ferraro, Vice President, Education and Consumer Products; and Carol LeBlanc, Senior Vice
President, Education and Consumer Products.

Image Credits
Alamy: Pictures Now, 16, Science History Images, 13 (top); Canadian Intellectual Property Office, 11;
Granger, 22; Library of Congress, 5, 12, 13 (bottom), 17, 24 (top), 25; National Archives and Records
Administration, 18; Newscom: World History Archive, 9; Shutterstock: Billion Photos, 4, Chones, 27, Everett
Art, 6, Everett Historical, cover (right), 7, 14, 15 (top), 24 (bottom), 28, 29, Georgios Kollidas, 8, James Steidl,
26 (right), overcrew, 26 (left), Sheila Fitzgerald, 23, Supachai Sumrubsuk, cover (left); SuperStock: Pantheon,
15 (bottom), 19, Science and Society, 10, 20

Design Elements by Shutterstock

Printed in the United States of America.
PA70

TABLE OF CONTENTS

INTRODUCTION

Click! That's the sound of a light bulb turning on. Light bulbs provide light. They are found in homes, offices, and schools. Thanks to inventor Thomas Edison, light bulbs are used all around the world today.

Most homes in the United States use about 45 light bulbs.

Thomas Edison was one of the most famous inventors in the world.

SOURCES OF LIGHT

For thousands of years, people lived without electricity. They used fire for light. Candles and oil lamps helped people see in the dark. But that type of light could be dangerous.

Before light bulbs, people used candles for light in their homes.

FLYING A KITE IN A STORM

Benjamin Franklin was curious about electricity. One day in 1752, he experimented during a thunderstorm. He tied a key onto a string. The string was attached to a kite. The string got wet. It picked up the electrical charge from the storm. Franklin kept working with electricity. He wanted to understand its uses.

Benjamin Franklin was an important leader in the early days of the United States. He was also an inventor.

ARC LAMPS

Many inventors tried to use electricity for light. They created different types of light bulbs. Sir Humphry Davy invented the electric arc lamp in the early 1800s. It was an electric battery connected to two carbon sticks. It was too bright for everyday use.

The arc lamp was very bright. It could light a whole street!

Sir Humphry Davy

arc lamp

ARC LAMPS AND INCANDESCENT LIGHTS

An arc lamp is made with two carbon sticks. Light is produced by a spark. The spark jumps between the two sticks. The lamp needs a battery or generator. An incandescent bulb needs electricity. The electric current runs through a filament. The filament is a strip of material that gets hot. When it is hot enough, it glows.

Today's incandescent light bulbs use a material called tungsten as the filament.

EARLY LIGHT BULBS

In the mid–1800s, Sir Joseph Wilson Swan worked on a light bulb. He spent years trying different ideas. His incandescent bulb used carbonized paper. But it would not stay lit very long.

Swan's electric lamp

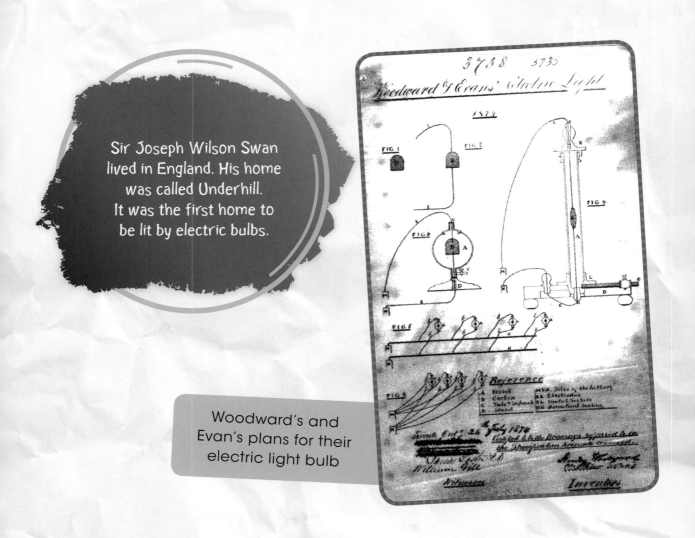

Sir Joseph Wilson Swan lived in England. His home was called Underhill. It was the first home to be lit by electric bulbs.

Woodward's and Evan's plans for their electric light bulb

Henry Woodward and Mathew Evans worked on a light bulb. They lived in Canada. They got a patent for their invention. Later they sold the patent to Thomas Edison.

A YOUNG INVENTOR

Thomas Edison was born on February 11, 1847, in Milan, Ohio. He was a curious child. He liked to see how things worked. He tested and tinkered with many ideas.

As a young man, Edison worked as a telegraph operator. He was curious about how the telegraph worked. He wanted to send messages more easily. He invented an automatic telegraph. It could send messages faster than before.

Edison at age 14

Edison's work as a telegraph operator sparked ideas for his inventions.

He also invented a "talking machine." It was known as the phonograph. It was the first machine to record and play back sound.

LEARNING AT HOME

Edison went to school for a few months. He was very bright. His teachers could not keep up with his ideas. His mother decided to teach him at home. She helped him with arithmetic and writing. She told him to read and learn new things.

"My mother was the making of me. She was so true, so sure of me; and I felt I had something to live for, someone I must not disappoint."

—Thomas Edison

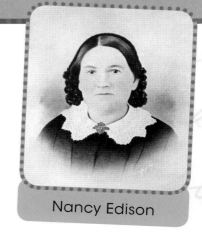

Nancy Edison

13

TEAMWORK

In 1876 Edison opened a laboratory. It was in Menlo Park, New Jersey. Edison hired a team of people. They all worked with him. They shared ideas for inventions. From 1878 to 1880, they worked on light bulbs. They improved the bulbs that others had created.

Edison

Edison and his team outside the Menlo Park laboratory in 1880

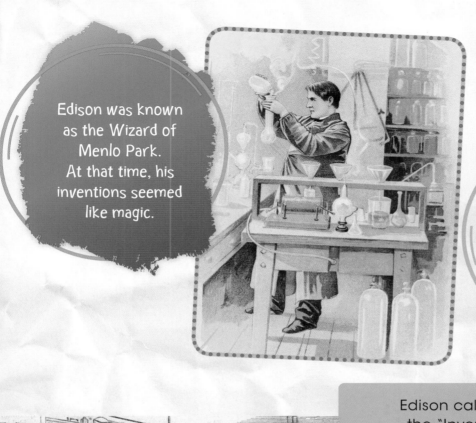

Edison was known as the Wizard of Menlo Park. At that time, his inventions seemed like magic.

Edison suffered hearing loss. He was partially deaf for most of his life.

Edison called Menlo Park the "Invention Factory."

For two years, Edison and his team experimented. They tried at least 3,000 different ideas. Their first bulbs were too bright. Others did not stay lit very long.

Edison tinkered with using just the right amount of electricity. His bulb was made of glass. It had a filament inside.

By the time he was in his 30s, Edison was one of the most famous men in the world.

FINDING A FILAMENT

Edison knew the filament was important. He needed to find the right material for it. He tried using platinum. One day he was rolling a piece of carbon between his fingers. That gave him an idea. He tried carbonizing different plants for the filament. He tried strips made of bamboo and wood. He tried linen, flax, and paper.

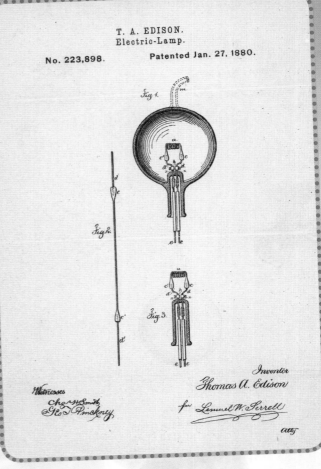

Edison's plans for the electric light bulb

"Before I got through, I tested no fewer than 6,000 vegetable growths and ransacked the world for the most suitable filament material."

—Thomas Edison

SUCCESS!

In 1879 Edison finally tried cotton thread as the filament. It stayed lit for nearly 14 hours. Edison had found the answer! The light bulb was ready for people to use in their homes.

Edison's filament lamp from 1879

TIMELINE OF THE LIGHT BULB

1752: Benjamin Franklin experiments with electricity during a storm.

EARLY 1800s: Sir Humphry Davy invents the first arc lamp.

1850s-1870s: Sir Joseph Wilson Swan works on a light bulb.

1874: Henry Woodward and Mathew Evans patent a light bulb.

1878: Thomas Edison begins experimenting with light bulbs.

1880: The light bulb is mass produced.

Edison started the Edison Electric Light Company. Business people invested in his company. This money helped Edison do his work. His company sold light bulbs to people. It sold bulbs to other businesses too.

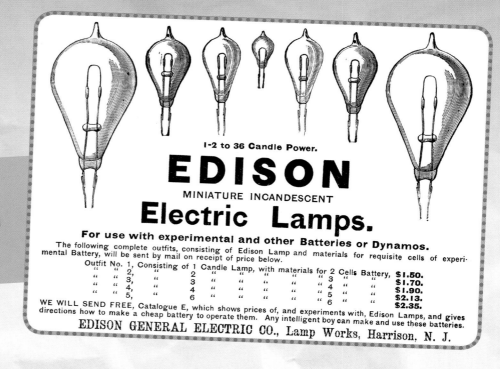

An ad for Edison's light bulbs appeared in a magazine in 1890.

The light bulb was successful. Other companies wanted to produce them. More electric companies were started. Eventually the Edison Electric Light Company joined another company. The two companies became General Electric. This company is still in business today.

New inventions are expensive! Edison was a good salesman. He asked investors to fund his work.

General Electric sells light bulbs and other products today.

LIGHTING HOMES AND NEIGHBORHOODS

Edison stands next to a dynamo, or generator. This Edison invention made electricity.

Edison continued his work with electricity. He invented an underground electrical system. He also set up a generator plant in New York City. His work brought light to homes, streets, and cities.

The Edison Electric lighting station was located on Pearl Street in New York City.

FAMOUS FUTURIST

Nikola Tesla was an inventor. He worked with Edison for a few months. He experimented with energy and electricity. After leaving Edison's company, Tesla designed the alternating current (AC) electricity system. This is the system still used today. Tesla said that wireless communication would one day be possible. He had big ideas for the future.

"Genius is one percent inspiration and ninety-nine percent perspiration."
—Thomas Edison

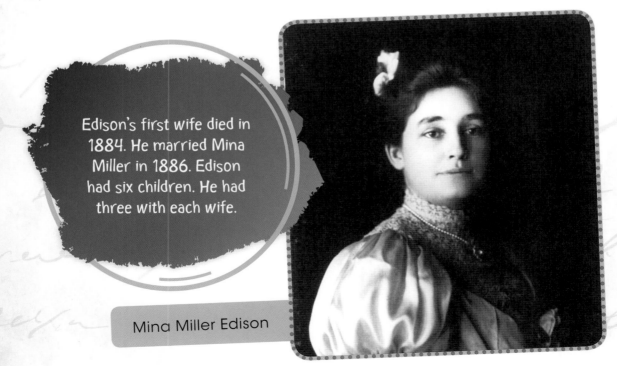

Edison's first wife died in 1884. He married Mina Miller in 1886. Edison had six children. He had three with each wife.

Mina Miller Edison

LIGHT BULBS TODAY

The light bulb has had many uses. Lights were added to cars. Then people could drive safely at night. Lights were added to cameras as flash bulbs. Today many homes use LED (light-emitting diode) lights. LED bulbs use less energy than incandescent bulbs. All of these inventions would not have been possible without Edison's discoveries.

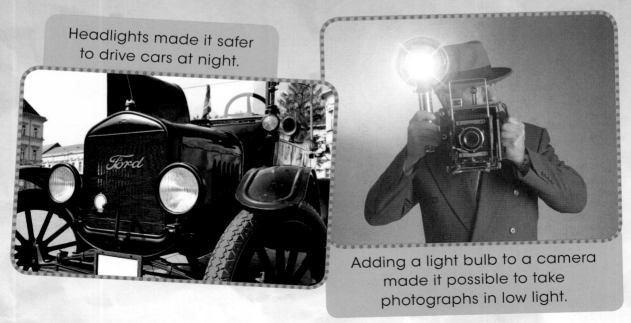

Headlights made it safer to drive cars at night.

Adding a light bulb to a camera made it possible to take photographs in low light.

Edison also created
the Edison screw.
It is the socket still
used for most light
bulbs today.

EDISON'S WORK

Edison had many ideas. He had 1,093 patents (alone or with other inventors). Some were for his work with electricity and light. Some were for his work with the phonograph and the telegraph. Others were for his work with batteries.

Thomas Edison died on October 18, 1931. He was buried in West Orange, New Jersey.

Edison in 1922

Edison invented the first movie machine in 1886.

Edison was one of the world's most important inventors. He is remembered for working with others to improve inventions. Today many people work on inventions together. His success was an early example of that teamwork.

Edison looks at a motion picture camera in 1925.

GLOSSARY

arc lamp—a lamp that uses an arc of electric current between two electrodes to produce light

carbon—an element found in all living things and in coal

charge—an amount of electricity running through something

filament—a thin wire or thread that lights or heats up with electricity

generator—a machine that provides electric energy

incandescent—describing a bulb that uses an electric current and filament to produce light

inventor—a person who thinks up and makes something new

invest—to provide funds to make more money through an invention or business

patent—a legal document giving someone sole rights to make or sell a product

phonograph—a machine that recorded and played back sound

platinum—a heavy grayish white metallic chemical element

telegraph—a system of sending messages over long distances that used wires and electrical signals

CRITICAL THINKING QUESTIONS

1. Why is it better for inventors to work as a team?

2. It usually takes many tries before an inventor succeeds. Explain why.

3. How important is it for inventors to experiment? Why?

READ MORE

Boone, Mary. *Thomas Edison: Physicist and Inventor.* North Mankato, MN: Capstone Press, 2018.

Demuth, Patricia Brennan. *Thomas Edison and His Bright Idea.* New York: Penguin Young Readers, 2016.

Scirri, Kaitlin. *Thomas Edison: Inventor and Innovator.* New York: Cavendish Square, 2020.

INTERNET SITES

The Franklin Institute: Edison's Lightbulb
http://www.fi.edu/history-resources/edisons-lightbulb

Thomas Edison National Historical Park
http://www.nps.gov/edis/index.htm

Thomas Edison's Inventive Life
http://invention.si.edu/thomas-edisons-inventive-life

INDEX